ne

Shag

Sue Vickerman has received three Arts Council (UK) awards for her poetry, novels and short stories. Shag, the first of her four poetry collections to date, was published during the half-decade she spent living in a Scottish lighthouse. An international readership follows Sue Vickerman's serialised biographical trilogy of 'Suki', failed poet and jobbing artist's model, at sukithelifemodel.co.uk. This is now available in print.

Home, says Sue Vickerman, is "wherever I hang my hat", but England's rugged post-industrial north - especially her native Yorkshire - always draws her back.

'Keenly observed birds punctuate the poems in this collection – all strong, straight-talking narratives. They are windows on worlds where various degrees of unsatisfactoriness are revealed. Birds or worlds, the essential mode is "watching" and Sue Vickerman's gaze is uncompromising, direct and wide-ranging; her language dense and gritty, at home on the edge of things.'
                Linda France, editor 'Sixty Women Poets' (Bloodaxe)

Also by Sue Vickerman

Poetry

The social decline of the oystercatcher,
Biscuit Publishing, England, 2005

Kunst by 'Suki', Indigo Dreams Publishing, England, 2012

Thin bones like wishbones by 'Suki' and Sue Vickerman,
Indigo Dreams Publishing, England, 2013

Fiction

Special needs, Cinnamon Press, Wales, 2011

A small life, Cinnamon Press, Wales, 2012

Two small lives, Naked Eye, England, 2016

Online fiction
asmalllife.co.uk
twosmalllives.co.uk
truelifenude.co.uk

Blog
sukithelifemodel.co.uk

SHAG

Sue Vickerman

Naked Eye Publishing

© Sue Vickerman 2003

All rights reserved

First published by Arrowhead Press 2003
Kindle edition published 2015
Naked Eye edition published 2017

Book design and typesetting by Naked Eye

ISBN: 1910981028
ISBN-13: 978-1910981023

www.nakedeyepublishing.co.uk

for Friederike

Acknowledgements

Thanks are due to the following publications in which some of these poems first appeared:

Orbis, The Yellow Crane, Rain Dog, Iota, Mslexia, Smiths Knoll, 'The Blue Room' Anthology (Diamond Twig, 1999), Lancaster Litfest Anthology (2001), Other Poetry, Coffee House, Cutting Teeth, The Affectionate Punch, 'The sensitively thin bill of the shag' Prizewinners' Anthology (Biscuit 2003).

Contents

The Sensitively Thin Bill Of The Shag 1
Older Women 2
First Time Out 3
Low Pressure 4
Love's Poem 5
Committing 6
Trelleborg to Sassnitz 7
Skylark 8
The Show Service 9
Fag-end 10
Father's Day 11
The Main Earner 12
The Gardening Section, B&Q 13
Afternoon Tea 14
Waiting for Puffins 15
Northern Sights 17
Looking for a sense of mystery 19
English Cathedral 20
Back Street 21
Apeshit 22
Chapel People 23
Leaving School 25
Weekend Break 26
Purple Sandpiper 27
The Fulmar 28
Richmond upon Thames 29
Back Where We Started 30
St Giles, Edinburgh 32
Stonehaven Harbour 33
The Black-backed Gull 34

The Sensitively Thin Bill Of The Shag

A squabble in the eaves, housemartins,
wakes us early. As I pour your breakfast tea
a gannet flop-glides off the lighthouse,
drops between smoke-rings of mist

while you swill spit from the basin,
put in your contacts, peer out at the tide
already lapping the slip-way, and I know
that you're going to shout *Heron! Let's go down.*

At the edge, where bladder-wrack stretches
skin-tight on the knees of boulders, where my boots
flatten pods and pick up slime, I remark
that the tide will isolate us if we're not careful

but you stride on, as usual, over thick kelp stipes,
shadows of fish in pools, liver-fleshed anemones,
and straddle the thin smile of a ravine, disregarding
the sea, how it foams your trainers into a wet shave,

how oyster-catchers clack their knitting-needle beaks
like wives complaining, and herring gulls line up,
laddish, on ledges. Your interest is only in exotic visitors.
Whinchat you call over wave-noise. *Or maybe a wheat-ear.*

Meanwhile, on a rock cling-wrapped in jelly-fish,
a solitary shag lands in a shallow glide, his posture
less refined than a cormorant, his loosely-crested nape
spiked, rakish, brave against the dashing water

and I notice him looking me over in a way you never do.
Steep-browed, thin bill; fine hook at the tip. When I skid,
blushing, on mustard-smeared granite, he winks,
shows me his profile, flexing his seaweed wings.

Older Women
A response to 'Men' by Kate Clanchy

I love their skin, crazed as an old dish,
their scent like freshly printed literature,
herb pillows, denim gone soft in the wash;
how they chop wood, take nostalgia trips
to Greenham, lift bikes up steps, do weights,
knit socks. I love the glimpse of private space
between shirt and skin, slacks on firm hips
from climbing in France. Women who drink Guinness
and wear rainbow woollies from Brazil, and embrace
other women; women whose positions on sex
are as relaxed as armchairs; women whose exes
are shelved in albums. They'll grab you like cake,
light your candles, lead you to believe,
then smile, put on their cycle clips and leave.

First Time Out
For Miriam and Ruth's noticeboard

Pausing for breath in Toxteth in a sea wind
you say you feel better. Last week's headlines
from the Echo unreel along derelict streets,
it's almost a movie except that the sky
is not painted, static. We watch it
slipping over itself like an oil-slick
gliding down-river, until you stop, look:

on a bench outside The Angel, women
without men play cards, flick ash, keep watch
on their buggies, give slaps. We catch the stench
of endless last rounds, lock-ins on dark nights,
then you frown, pull my arm, point
at the tar by your foot where a baby bird lies,
ribbed with bike tyres, cheek down.

From the bricked-up church, a chipped saint
is reaching out like a Big Issue seller
but beyond the brewery you see a bright stage-set
and we pass him by, hurry on to our destination,
strung-out lights, galleries, the marina where palms
wave from balconies and clustered yachts
chatter like extras. I toss change in a busker's hat
and get us icecreams, first of the season.

You know, we could move here if you wanted.
But the sky pulls you down, down to the edge of the quay
where a rail weathered to a hairgrip is all that keeps you
from the mud and shadow of the empty Mersey.
You remark on the beauty of distant lace-necked cranes
while I sense rain, notice pockmarks on the water's skin
and although you're smiling, I do up your coat.
You know we shouldn't stand here for very long.

Low Pressure

I said it would be stern as a school uniform,
dull as winter heather. But Aberdeen was gentle
as an egg-box, pencil-shaded, hesitant outlines
smudged by the weather; cock-eyed sea-birds perched
on cardboard cut-out turrets high above the shops
on Union Street, while heads wrapped up like sweets
bobbed by, and men strode down to the gaudy ships

where you, delighted, took snaps of the docks,
metallic red and blue blocked into sketched space.
I could live here, you said, lingering at the sight
of a papery warehouse blown empty. That night
on the coast road we parked under lowering cloud
and argued, while behind us in fading light, the city
mulched like papier-mâché beneath the press of granite.

Love's Poem
for Friederike

Love was planted in a niche
between two lands, when you answered
in my language, led me by the hand
into the Shanghai Hilton.

Love mushroomed in the steam of cooked rice,
crystallised with the onset of frost,
found us beneath a silk quilt in a guesthouse
in Guilin.

In love we zigzagged down a willow-pattern stream,
shared courtesy soaps, savoured everything for when
we couldn't be together, said Aufwiedersehen
until Berlin.

Then love heaved coal briquets up basement steps,
lit fires before daylight, took weekend trains
to Czech nightspots; love was spartan,
needs pared down to flesh.

Now that love has arrived in the restful greens
of England, rain falls daily while bread rises slowly,
and love dreams of forests, though the land is bare,
wide open.

Committing
With thanks to Rev Judy Sutterlin

On the day of the wedding in Xiamen
we slipped away as the tables were laid ready;
eloped, heading for the estuary.

We examined the sands, unsure of the right spot,
made an arbitrary stop facing China, facing
the incoming tide. We had no liturgy

so we gathered flotsam sticks, constructed
a lucky character on the unfamiliar territory,
made promises, held hands under a veil of rain

and almost forgot the ceremony. Racing the tide
we gathered up our double-happiness and returned,
too late, after the main entry, after the bride.

Trelleborg to Sassnitz

The radar of a small green lighthouse is spinning
across my porthole. You beckon me out to the deck, point
at a tousle of windmills on the headland as we dock
alongside the dark sinew of somewhere that isn't Dover,
the unwinding snake of another foreign territory.

In the phone-booth of the terminal, I clutch the faint question
in the receiver, picking with difficulty through currency
in your uncurling fist. Salt-lipped, you shift your rucksack
while the digital seconds flicker out, and my answer
no we're not in Berlin; *not yet,* gets cut to a single negative.

Skylark

A shaken-out blanket of yellow rape
makes us pull up, picnic-minded. I laugh
as a comic-strip hare bounces into a field
nippled with cut turnips, but you miss it

and then on our backs in the rumpled meadow
I hear it first: the spiralling phrases,
the rising hover of the classic aerial singer,
piece of grit swimming over my eyeball,
a flicker in the chlorine sky. *Look*
I indicate the particle against the sun,
the speck on the blue screen of August

but you find the skylark sharp-tongued, shrill
as a kettle, its vibrato making you shiver,
sanding your sockets like migraine,
its ultimate plunge splitting your head.

The Show Service

The sermon was all about belonging. Later, arm in arm
the vicar and her lover stroll away from the marquee

shaking old men's hands beneath the evening sun. The calm
unchanging face of the land goes misty when Abide With Me

floats across the years from the silver band. The farmers see
only the sobriety of her robes, a celibate vocation thriving,

blind to the intimate touch of the girl who does the driving.

Fag-end

When his watch
catches her ear-ring
and a pigeon lands
by her shoulder

when the obelisk gesticulates
like a cigarette
and she smells nicotine
under his nails

when the day
slackens off, pink-skyed,
and he walks away
across the cemetery

she necks the bottle
for the dregs
when a trickle of something
penetrates

when she gets up
from the wet soil
but can't find
her kicked-off shoes.

Father's Day

Waiting in the porch for the organ, sweating already,
trying to scratch under my collar, then she's faffing
with my damned cravat. I tell her *walk steady.*

She straightens my carnation, hands over my hat
and I know she can't wait for her feet up with a fag,
watching the video later, back at the flat.

We head off. Everyone's taking snaps, then that slag
she works with comes out in the aisle for a good view,
takes a full frontal, winks at the padre who smiles,

the fool, while the wife cries in the front pew
in a hat from another wedding – daylight robbery
and they've split up already – but the jacket's new.

Of course, the vicar's part of a racket, making a bob
or two by dressing like a prat, but it's a grand morning
for flowers, left from yesterday's funeral (Almighty God,
you noticed my pocket) and now here's kick-off: that reading,
the one that goes *Love is...* Hell. Always the same reading.

The Main Earner

The kettle's not on.
His toes, their necks stretched
through holes, smile up in the firelight.

You didn't do the washing.
As she pulls off her jacket, a whole shift's
scraped plates whets his appetite.

Sink full of pots…
He dabs ash into a tea-cup,
undoes his flies while she peels down her tights.

Put the telly on.
The settee scuffs the wall-paper
as they copulate, bickering, in the blue light.

Stop, it's the Lottery.
He flicks from a cartoon to the right channel
as she untangles her knickers.

They've put me on earlys.
He licks a Rizla, snaps open a Bud-lite
while she microwaves burgers and fries.

Midnight till eight thirty.
She watches him lighting the joint, how the flare
of the twist on the end lights up his soft, dewy eyes.

The Gardening Section, B&Q

She's leaving the last aisle of home-improvement
with a bedroomy lightshade in her trolley
to replace the only thing
he ever said he liked.
The day he left
she chucked it.

All aisles lead to the outdoor world of gardening
where the floor will turn into soft earth
and her heels will no longer catch
on scattered shavings
from the cut wood
of pine doors.

Turning the end, her hips already nudging on Gro-bags
piled high as trees, she hears that the circular saw
is currently manned and turning, and turning
she feels the stranger's look, as soil
pulls water down into itself
drawing her in.

Afternoon Tea

Shopping on a narrow street
she stops to check her hat,
hot-flushes,
goes for cakes.

He pulls on her frocks,
checks in the mirror,
sees an angel. Later
she rehangs them properly.

A blazing fire
burns on her cheek
when she offers cake
and he replies *you're an angel.*

Waiting for Puffins

You said they would arrive in May.
Noticing a gossamer of droppings
cobwebbed over the cliffs, sheer rock
feathered into a duvet, my hopes soar
out of the window. I forfeit a cooked breakfast
for seaweed and scrambled pudding-stone,
locking the lighthouse but leaving a note
just in case: *Gone to puffins. You know where.*

Scanning the chess-board of sleek-backed auks
I train your loaned binoculars on profiles,
rubbing the steam of my hot look from your lenses,
trying to catch a distinctive beak, curious
eye-markings, tell-tale red among grey suits
of kittiwakes. A thick-set fulmar hangs stiff-winged
on an updraught, stalls, then drops. Guillemots,
startled, unfurl overhead. I dodge, umbrella-ed.

Auks need ledges on which to rest, whereas puffins
dig burrows in the soft ground of cliff tops.

My boots catch on lichen, slip in pools
while the rising tide pulls slowly at the time
available, slides round another inlet. I clamber
beyond common sense, sure of a sighting,
the distinctively large head, the amusing waddle.
Scaling the milk-stained cliff among the waterfalls
of nests, I reach the final outcrop, and discover
an inaccessible bay, curved in a lipless smile.

There! I zoom in, breathless, on a patch like liquorice,
touching the focus lightly, waiting for a profile
that doesn't jab and point. I blink back salt,
blink away my double-vision, a thousand couplings.
But there are no bright, calypso beaks, jolly as plastic;
no sad-eyed, comical sea-birds from book-spines
and cartoons, the ones you promised; only auks'
dark looks and razorbills' blunt chins, and my eye-
corners lapped by the encroaching edge of the sea.

Northern Sights
For a German friend newly blinded

I Manchester Airport

I planned to tell you about the turbanned men
reading The Times while waiting; a Jamaican
in charge of the catering, Hasidic Jews
flocked at the Lunn Poly stand;
an espresso bar where bacon slivers
visible along the cutline of baguettes
don't smell at all, though in fact this
is England where we eat bacon for breakfast.
But your stick tap-dances over my rehearsal,
avoiding objects, except that you say
coffee smells the same, and I accept
that the rush of air as you landed was universal
and our rain will have more effect on your stay
than the promise of an Indian take-away.

II Beer

Your cheeks are glass. The storm dashes down
the dale, down your face until you perceive
the moor like a skylight, thrashed with sleet.
Arriving at the Old Silent, drowned,
you turn down a pint. I buy a round
for one. Your salad arrives un-dressed,
so English, but in the end, lettuce is lettuce,
drifting from your fork without a sound,
fluttering from your plate to the ground.
Heading home on the bus your reflection
still shines wet. I change the subject, ask
whether anything else leads you to believe
that this is England. Sheep, you say.
Later, I order an Indian take-away.

III Curry

I try to empathise, dutifully,
suffer that violent red-green lightshow
in your head, but I see a rainbow,
and say nothing as it fades beautifully
like the line of your cheek against green
as we passed wild garlic, or when I saw
the fell glowing red behind your jaw.
You gasp, sharp as a lens zooming in,
tasting Madras, a gentle fold of naan bread
in your hands. For now, I'll turn your head
with picked lilac, but later I'll persuade you
to spend autumn here: sit close
to the fire, taste coal, feel twilight crocheted
round the village, smell northern dusk.

Looking for a sense of mystery

in the rust trickling from the Saxon arch's
upside-down smile; the melted way
the chancel steps dip; the clatter of a pigeon
in the rafters; an angel depicted in mildew.

At the exit, returning my ten pence history,
I hear an echo below the belfry and come upon
a sarcophagus broken open, undated,
its inside egg-shell dry, boneless, vacated.

English Cathedral

I make the sign, genuflect, belong.
You whisper for the exit but I linger
browsing, Marks & Spencers-style, among
the classical, the quality. I finger
and admire, buy a candle at the altar.
The cafe in the crypt is made of pews.
I wax lyrical, while you falter:
This is cream tea. This is the news
according to the BBC. This is cricket.
I was born while Last Night of the Proms
was on TV, grew up going on picnics
in all weathers, knew every Python song

while you grew into purdah, grew discreet
at the same school, on the same street.

Back Street

It comes in rubies
beautiful as the violet slit
of the lamb's throat
a halal slaughter

squatting over the toilet
in the dying moments
I pull my chador over my head
as a mark of respect

I am a dutiful daughter.

Apeshit

Every single kid on our estate
is watching two baboons on our front path

and I'm running away with your cricket bat –
let's go down the rec. You bring the wickets
as some of my mam's hair floats by on the wind.

Bitch you bitch – big arse in red pants,
your mam on top, kicking, while up in the air
are my mam's gorilla slippers.

Chapel People

Dedicated to the late Rev. John Rigby, and all the Methodist ministers in my address book.

Whispered prayers would always sound historical,
the way they came out, dry as parchment
and fluttered along the pews, shifting dust
in the limited light. Disciples' robes
in high windows would mottle our hands,
and when collection money accidentally
jigged out of pockets during a hymn
we'd stamp on the rolling coins,
and we'd squint at the pulpit, the glare
of a broad satin tie, fist glancing off wood,
hearing about the sick, the dead, the fighting
everywhere, and we'd kick at black knots
in the panelling during the Children's Address,
sniffing at Victorian stains on the cloth-bound bibles
under our chins while Sunday School Assistants
in mini-skirts, surreptitiously untwizzling Fox's
Glacier Mints, hissed in our ears, their pink knees
nudging our backs, until somebody finally
answered the preacher's question with Jesus.

* * *

One day we were singing
Blessed Be The Ties That Bind
when John the Baptist ran in,
shouting, followed by his dog.
Shit-matted sheep's tails
dangled from his scalp
and a studded belt
clung to his whippet loins.

He was stoned and grinning,
his DMs laced with string,
chains strung between his piercings,
a puncture in his eyebrow.
He must be up from London
we all said. Anyway,
he vaulted into the sanctuary
hollering like Tarzan
and bared his concave chest.
You could see he never ate.
He was dragging a blanket.
A patchouli aura spread
like God's body odour.
He grabbed the collection plate,
shouted Stuff God! then stuffed
his pockets with our offering,
farted, and legged it, with his dog.
An urban prophet, we all said.

* * *

The way the plastic neck twizzles out of the bread-bin
brings back Fox's mints, as our spinster aunt,
the only surviving organist, pulls at the Sunblest's
soft head and drops it into her wheely-basket,
stillborn. Her bad legs suffer along the via dolorosa:
down the snicket by the factory, up the back steps
of the chapel that smells of all our childhoods
and into the vestry where, laying the loaf on the slab,
she carries out the act. Slice, then cube; slice…
Her accustomed hands assemble the crumbs
on a silver plate to be offered round like buns at a wake
to the gathered few. And watching them partake,
whether out of habit, or for old times' sake, or in case
it really does mean eternal life, brings back Jesus.

Leaving School

From the staffroom the moor rises beyond the playground,
handsome as a strong jaw grizzled with weather. They trickle
from the gate to their flaking housing shaved out of the fell
except for, way up, a farm piled like dark muck on heather.

The Ovenden road is a boot laced with powerlines, scuffed
by foul winds, dog-messed. We mumble destinations,
heads down, escaping, while tattooed windows stare out the bus
til it leaves, a Morrison's bag hooked like skin on its wiper.

By the time we reach Cullingworth one man has emerged
light-hearted from his woolly hat and wound-round scarf,
who only works over that way, and who has teacher friends
who are stressed. The glass is lacquered with warm breath

and gay with villagey lights, and we all pity that estate
slouched like a smoker in the gloom of another valley.

Weekend Break

When we pulled up at dusk in nylony rags
of yellow mist, Pendle Hill looked veined and bulbous.
Fine drizzle mellowed your complexion.

After the B & B, bloated, we stretched our legs
in the vicinity. The swollen hill ebbed into the land
like a corpse, seepage pulling at our boots.

We tried to picnic, but each time the sun shone
the contours turned into candlewick
rumpled on twisting bones.

On the hunched bridge in the long evening light,
feeling the hill on our backs like thunder,
we saw our shadows mount the parapet

and hover above the rich pulp of decay.
I crept into the dark cleft of your chin
like a cave, out of sight, afraid,
narrowing my perspective to your profile.

Purple Sandpiper

I lead you to the real beauties: brown
on beige; blue on blue like gulls' eggs,
or buffish, the eggs of the common tern
mottled with olive. The colours of Scotland.
After they dry, they'll be as disappointing
as the slate-brown of a purple sandpiper.
But even as you speak, a wave shifts
more precious finds towards my toes.
They are too big for your pockets; too wet.
Too heavy for the car. So I take snaps
of the best: pearl-skinned; unblemished
as the horizon; rough-smooth as your face.

Blue morning, November, another country.
When I hear the pack of photos drop in the hall,
pond-still, I turn to your beige pillow, slide
my hand through your chilled space, grey on grey.

Finally, in May, I purchase a book: slate-brown,
its pages the colour of bones. My beauties
will soon shimmer like a holiday, like treasure
rediscovered, in an album entitled 'Stones'.

The Fulmar

That morning, a keen wind sliced
the cake-edge of Scotland and the tide
whisked rocks into shortbread crumbs
and swelled and melted like meringue
as I held your ladder at the lighthouse window.
You tucked and poked into draughts
with a Swiss knife, denim braced
against glass, while blizzard conditions
sugared the cliffs, beat the headland
into peaked egg-whites, made gateau
of the scenery as ducktape unreeled
around our circular rooms, sealing us in.

You saw the fulmar first, thick-set,
steering heavily against the wind.
Like an albatross, I warned. An omen.
You only laughed, loving his bulk;
his lecherous, bull-necked look.
Meanwhile the fire in our hearth, lit
by a small match before breakfast,
roared, unchecked, until it ignited
the chimney; until blue flames
leapt from the top of our tall house
like a pudding *flambé*, alerting ships
to the treacherous nature of the territory.

Richmond upon Thames

At last you drop your rucksack
like an anchor, and we're here:
breathing herbs, dappled by period glass,
a rainbow playing on your face
as you pull on embroidered slippers
(one of your Dad's trips; Kashkar)
while your mother calls hello, cobwebbed
in her studio sketching roses
she caught earlier in the garden
where they'd been running wild.

You tip out a new loaf in the kitchen
while your brother, in a blazer with a crest
involving Latin, picks up a decanter,
croons something French, pours wine.
Très bien I reply, pushing my gift, olives
in polystyrene, behind the cafétière.
Somewhere, a violin is rehearsing
as we slide odd plates, napkin rings,
ornate knives, across the cloth.

Later you show me your playroom:
a piano, a watercolour nude
between willow switches in a vase,
your surname by his foot. I swirl my fingers
in the dust on the mahogany
until my name appears. *We need a cleaner*
you grin, sifting your semester of mail,
spinning a globe with your satin toe
as I grip my cuff, sweep the piano
with the functional cloth of my whole arm.

Back Where We Started

That smell again. The Tyne
is a skidmark on un-ironed wasteland,
the damp-linen sky rucked in piles
above the bridge where I scrape off
the side of my shoe.

Shivering by Wesley's obelisk
we eat bagels, swig wine
and you marvel at the changes,
the tipped-out Meccano of trucks,
cranes scavenging in muck
on the Gateshead bank.

The quayside is serrated.
You lead me on a knife-edge
to the kind of bar you love, café latte
and jaffa tart, lightly warmed, sexy.
I pick off specks of cinnamon
while you sip gin, frustrated.

At the next table, her drink is a double.
The sly neck, that diamante grin
winking in the eye of your cuff-link
makes you wish we still lived here,
whereas my smile glances sharply
off the dead-faced river, and I think
I can hear rats in the rubble.

Walking back up Grey Street
the sky is an icepack on a migraine
but you're oblivious, lost in the Bolivian band
that still plays on the steps at Monument

but the singer is now a Goth, and their clothing
is no longer a rainbow but black on black
and the office where our eyes first met
on the early shift has become a tapas bar.

I stand apart, not wanting to throw money
in that hat, not wanting to be back here
when around the square
the echoes have totally changed.

St Giles, Edinburgh
for Frieder Sommer

I was there, next to the pigeoned monument
in front of St Giles at the time we arranged.
I watched the large, pale hats of a wedding
mushroom in the entrance, scanned the tour groups
for your beard. A minstrel, emerald green and red,
shook the bells of his three-cornered head-dress
at a child, grinned, and struck up a Beatles medley
while the photographer's tripod pranced on the steps
of the cathedral, and foreigners snapped Scotland:
the bride; the Rolls; men in kilts lighting cigarettes.

When you didn't come, I looked for another entrance
round the side, searching the spiked wig of scaffolding.
'Scotland The Brave' brought me back to the monument,
but the piper stopped to scratch his knee and check
his watch, and his instrument lost its breath and died,
while the minstrel's electric guitar gently wept.

Stonehaven Harbour

We could do that. But your dark glasses look,
instead, out to sea. I say *Maybe*. The yacht-clubbers
on the slip-way zip each other into black rubber
then step nimbly, suction-soled, banana-skinned,
onto perspex. Their silhouettes link, seamless
then part, like mime artists, dodging the swing of the sail.

Taking my ice-cream from you I feel it again,
the bullet-sized piece of knowledge triggered
by my reaching arm; the small knot of fear
in my breast, 'non-urgent', assigned to the slow list.
We float by the Marine Hotel, the Ship Inn,
a backpack laid out on the harbour wall, hikers
from Germany, a gang of over-sixties friends.
White sails kite over the water; a child complains;
the golden retriever swims slowly back to base
with the stick. Waiting is hardest at weekends.

The Black-backed Gull

After you'd gone, I returned to the beach one day
with a Tesco's bag, picked plastics out of the jaw
of the wide-mouthed cave, extracted bottles
from the line of chewed flotsam. Flies, disturbed
from seaweed nests, complained around my head
and a gannet came close then plunge-dived
between the waves rushing at my boots.

Finally all the unnatural colours were collected
in my carrier. Hearing a cry, I turned to face
the cove's dry throat and saw a Macdonalds-red
slit neck staining the bric-a-brac left by the tide,
the lemon-fizz bill of a puffin. I scanned the cliffs,
aimed rocks at the dog-bark of the murderous
black-backed gull: *Get away. Go. Get away.*

After restoring the cove to shades of grey,
to how it was with you, I heard the cry again
and, looking back, found myself whisker-close
to the past; to the hollow, widowed eyes of a seal.

Naked Eye Publishing

A fresh approach to publishing

Naked Eye Publishing is part of the revolution. We embody the newly levelled playing field, sidestepping the publishing establishment to produce beautiful books by and for creatives, intellectuals, art-lovers and bookworms at an affordable price, not profit-motivated. We also publish downloadable versions of all of our books, if feasible. Writers we publish do not need agents, do not have to financially invest, and do benefit from free global availability and distribution through our printing firm's worldwide partnerships – not least Barnes and Noble, Bertrams, Gardners, Waterstones and Amazon. Using the most up-to-date print technology we publish books of old-fashioned good quality.

nakedeyepublishing.co.uk

www.ingramcontent.com/pod-product-compliance
Lightning Source LLC
Chambersburg PA
CBHW071323080526
44587CB00018B/3333